Discover It Yourself

Plants and Flowers

KINGFISHER

LONDON & NEW YORK

T0014714

KINGFISHER
LONDON & NEW YORK

Copyright © Macmillan Publishers
International Ltd 2001, 2022, 2024
Published in 2022
This edition published in 2024
in the United States by Kingfisher,
120 Broadway, New York, NY 10271
Kingfisher is an imprint of Macmillan
Children's Books, London
All rights reserved.

Distributed in the U.S. and Canada by
Macmillan, 120 Broadway, New York,
NY 10271

EU representative: Macmillan
Publishers Ireland Limited, 1st Floor,
The Liffey Trust Centre, 117-126
Sheriff Street Upper, Dublin 1,
D01 YC43

Designed by: Tall Tree
Written by: Sally Morgan
Illustrated by: Diego Vaisberg/
Advocate Art

Material previously published in
Young Discoverers Plant Life (2001)

ISBN: 978-0-7534-7766-3 (HB)
978-0-7534-7768-7 (PB)

Libraray of Congress
Catalogining-in-Publication data
has been applied for.

Kingfisher books are available for
special promotions and premiums.
For details contact: Special Markets
Department, Macmillan, 120
Broadway, New York, NY 10271.

For more information, please visit
www.kingfisherbooks.com

Printed in China
9 8 7 6 5 4 3 2 1
1TR/0224/WKT/128MA

Contents

Make sure you have a grown-up to help whenever you see this sign.

All Kinds of Plants

There are over 390,000 different kinds of plants, and they are found in all but the very coldest parts of Earth. There are plants in the ocean, too. We recognize most plants easily because they are green. The color comes from green pigment called chlorophyll. Plants range in size from tiny single-celled algae to giant redwoods and Australian eucalyptus trees that reach more than 330 feet (100 m) tall. Some plants live for just a few weeks, and others live for thousands of years.

Tallest Plants

The giant redwoods of California are some of the tallest plants in the world, reaching heights of more than 330 feet (100 m).

Seaweeds

Seaweeds are marine plants that do not have true roots and stems. They have a root-like structure called a holdfast that attaches to rocks, and fronds that bend with the currents.

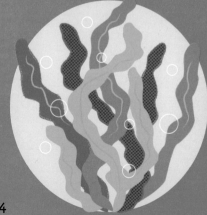

Conifer

Moss

Eye Spy

Many different types of plants can be found in parks and gardens. Try to find an example of a plant from the groups listed below when you are outside.

Plants can be divided into groups. Algae, which include seaweeds, are the simplest plants. Mosses and ferns are primitive land plants. Conifers are a group of large, cone-bearing plants. The most advanced plants are the flowering plants. Their flowers produce seeds and fruit. They include the broad-leaved trees.

Broad-leaved tree

Flowering plant

Parts of a Plant

Each flowering plant has a shoot with stems and leaves and a root system under the ground. Flowers are produced at certain times of the year and when pollinated can turn into fruits and seeds.

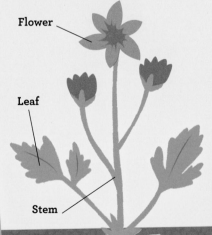

Flower

Leaf

Stem

Root

Making Their Own Food

Plants are different from other living organisms because they make their own food by photosynthesis. This process takes place in the leaves, where there is plenty of chlorophyll. Some photosynthesis also takes place in green stems. Plants have many leaves to trap as much light as possible. During the day the chlorophyll absorbs light energy from the Sun. This is used to turn carbon dioxide and water into sugar—which is used to fuel the plant's growth—and oxygen. Sometimes the sugar is stored as starch. The oxygen is released into the air. Oxygen is needed by animals and plants.

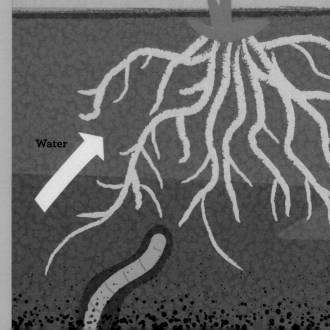

Carbon dioxide

Water

Eye Spy

Compound

Simple

Prickly

Not all leaves look the same. There are simple, compound, and prickly leaves. Compound leaves have several leaflets. Look for different leaf shapes and draw them in a notebook.

Largest Leaves

The huge floating leaves of the giant water lily are the world's largest simple leaves, often reaching 6.5 feet (2 m) across. They are supported by ribs that extend out from the center. The leaves are so strong that they can support the weight of a young child.

DISCOVER IT YOURSELF!

See how a green bean plant seeks the light.

1. Put a green bean seed in a container of potting soil. Water the soil and wait for the seed to grow.

2. Take a shoe box with a lid and cut a hole in one end. Paint the inside of the box and the lid with black paint.

3. Using smaller pieces of cardboard, position some "shelves" as shown in the diagram.

4. Stand the box so that the hole is at the top. Put the green bean plant inside and replace the lid.

5. Every few days, open the box and water the plant.

? How It Works

The green bean plant detects the dim light coming through the hole and grows toward it. Plants make sure that their leaves are in the best position for photosynthesis.

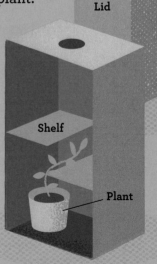

Lid

Shelf

Plant

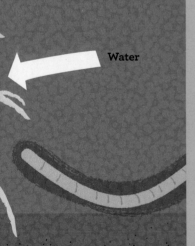

Sunlight

Oxygen

Water

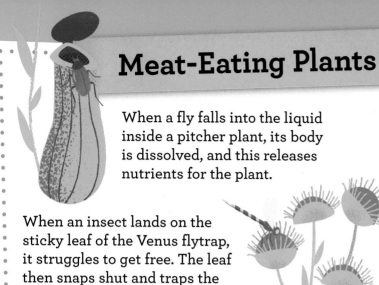

Meat-Eating Plants

When a fly falls into the liquid inside a pitcher plant, its body is dissolved, and this releases nutrients for the plant.

When an insect lands on the sticky leaf of the Venus flytrap, it struggles to get free. The leaf then snaps shut and traps the insect inside.

Light is essential for plants—without it they would become yellow and stop growing. They also need nutrients from the soil, especially nitrogen, phosphorus, and potassium. Farmers make sure that plants get enough nutrients by adding fertilizers to the soil. Fertilizers contain balanced amounts of nutrients to get the best possible growth from the crops.

One way to make sure that plants get enough nutrients is to add decaying plants or manure to the soil. This is mixed into the soil so that the plants' roots can absorb the nutrients.

Eye Spy

Not all leaves are green. Make a note of the different colored leaves of plants in your home. Some plants from tropical countries have red pigments for protection against the strong sun.

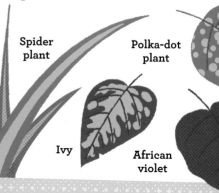

Spider plant

Polka-dot plant

Ivy

African violet

Leaf Mosaics

The leaves of a tree are carefully arranged in a mosaic pattern so that they do not shade each other.

Changing Color

In the fall, the leaves of deciduous trees change color from green to shades of yellow and red as the chlorophyll breaks down. Finally, the leaves drop. New green leaves form from buds in the spring.

DISCOVER IT YOURSELF!

Discover how important nutrients are to the growth of plants.

1. Fill a small tub or pot with sand. Fill another tub with sand mixed with a teaspoonful of slow-release fertilizer. Firm the sand in each tub with your hand. Water both.

2. Sprinkle grass seed evenly and cover with a thin layer of sand. Place the tubs on a sunny window ledge and water them regularly if they dry out.

3. Measure the height of the grass each week and compare the color of the leaves.

? How It Works

Sand on its own does not contain nutrients, so the grass growing in just sand will not grow well. The leaves will be yellow and short. Fertilizer provides grass with nutrients, so it will grow taller and the leaves will be a healthy green.

Tub with sand

Tub with fertilizer and sand

Roots

Roots hold a plant firmly in the ground and absorb water and nutrients from the soil. Some plants, such as dandelions, have a sturdy tap root that extends deep into the ground. Others, such as grasses, have a network of fibrous roots that spread out around the plant. Just behind the tip of each root is a group of tiny root hairs. These allow the roots to reach a wide area to absorb as much water as possible. Some roots are used to store food, such as starch. When this happens, the roots swell up and become tubers.

Deepest Roots

Roots can extend deep into the ground to find water. The deepest roots ever measured reached a depth of 400 feet (120 m). They belonged to a wild fig tree growing in South Africa.

Eye Spy

When you next visit the grocery store, see how many vegetables there are that come from the root of a plant.

Dandelion (tap root)

Dahlia (tuber)

Underground Storage

Some roots and bulbs become swollen as sugar is moved to the roots and stored as starch. The plant uses this food supply in the spring to send up new leaves and flowers. Many of these roots are foods we eat, and the flowers can tell us when the food is ready to be harvested.

Beet

Cassava

Onion

Ginger

Radish

Grass (fibrous root)

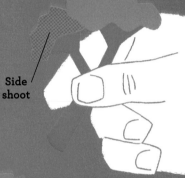

1. Break off a side shoot where it joins the main stem.

Side shoot

2. Stand the shoot in water and leave it on a window ledge until roots have grown.

Water

Roots

3. Plant the rooted shoot in a small pot of soil. Place a plastic bag around the pot to keep the air moist and watch your new plant grow.

Inside a Plant

Plants have to be able to move water and food from the roots to the leaves, and from the leaves to the growing tips. Inside a plant there is a system of tubes. Water is absorbed by the roots and is moved through tubes, called xylem, up the stem to the leaves. When the water reaches the leaves, some is used in photosynthesis, but most evaporates from the surface of the leaves. This process is called transpiration. Sugar is carried in tubes, called phloem, from the leaves to wherever it is needed for growth. Sugar can be moved both up and down the plant, whereas water moves only one way.

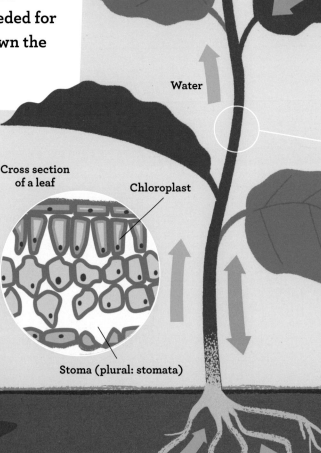

Sugar

Water

Cross section of a leaf

Chloroplast

Stoma (plural: stomata)

Beech

Laurel

Transpiration

If a plant loses too much water, it wilts. A beech leaf loses far more water than a laurel leaf, which has a waxy, waterproof upper surface.

DISCOVER IT YOURSELF!

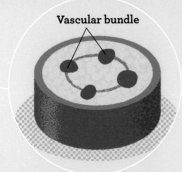

Color a flower by putting it in water with food coloring.

1. Carefully split the stem of a white flower, such as a carnation.

2. Support the flower so that one part of the stem is in blue-colored water and the other is in red water.

3. Gradually the veins in the white petals will become colored.

During the day, water evaporates from the surface of leaves. Trees have thousands of leaves, and the largest trees can lose as much as 265 gallons (1,000 L) of water each day.

DISCOVER IT YOURSELF!

Leaf rubbings make interesting pictures.

1. Lay a leaf face up on a table. Put a piece of white paper on top.

2. Using the side of a crayon, rub over the leaf so that the pattern of the veins is visible on the paper.

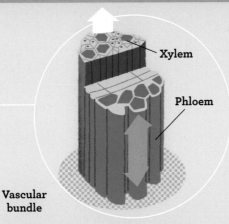

Vascular bundle

Xylem

Phloem

Section through the stem

Vascular bundle

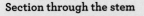

A network of tubes connects all the parts of the plant. In the stem, the phloem and xylem are close together in the vascular bundle. These bundles form the veins in leaves. When water reaches the leaves, some enters the chloroplast to be used in photosynthesis, but most of the water evaporates from the surface of the leaves. Water from the xylem moves through the air spaces in the leaves and out through holes called stomata.

Plants are essential to the survival of all living things. They are called producers because they are responsible for making food. Animals are consumers because they eat plants or other animals for food. Some animals, called herbivores, eat only plants. Other animals, called carnivores, eat the herbivores. Omnivores eat both plants and animals. In this way, plants and animals form food chains. If anything happened to the plants, there would not be enough food for the herbivores and they would starve. So would the carnivores and omnivores.

Plants have ways of protecting themselves from herbivores. Touching poison ivy may cause an itchy skin rash. Some trees have thorns, and nettles are protected by stinging leaves.

DISCOVER IT YOURSELF!

Dead leaves and plant matter can be broken down into compost.

!

1. Shape some wire mesh into a circle and support it with four wooden canes.

2. Line the structure with sheets of newspaper. Place your food and garden waste inside.

3. Cover the top with a piece of old carpet and leave for a few months.

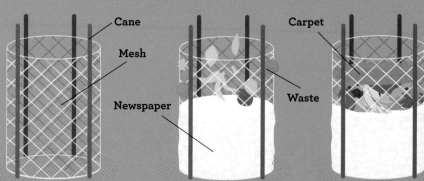

Cane

Mesh

Newspaper

Carpet

Waste

? How It Works

As tiny organisms start to break down the plant material, they release a lot of heat. The carpet and newspaper help trap the heat, speeding up the breaking-down process. After a few months, you should have a rich organic compost that can be put back into the soil.

Full circle

Plants need nutrients for healthy growth. Luckily, these nutrients are recycled, so they never run out. The remains of plants and animals are broken down by bacteria and fungi, and the nutrients are returned to the soil.

15

Plants as Food

Plants are an important source of food, and they make up a large part of our diet. The three most important plants are rice, corn, and wheat. These plants are large grasses called cereals. Cereals are useful plants because they produce seeds that contain starch and protein that we need. Wheat seeds are ground up to make flour, while rice and corn can be cooked as they are. All over the world, people survive on a largely vegetarian diet that contains lots of plants and very little animal food.

Rice

Wheat

Corn

Most of the world's richest soils are used for growing cereal crops. Cereals are often grown in huge fields, and the crops are collected by enormous combines.

Scientists look for better ways of growing crops. These tomatoes receive a mixture of nutrients to ensure maximum growth.

Plants as Medicine

For thousands of years plants have been used to reduce pain, heal wounds, and cure illnesses. The bark of the cinchona tree produces quinine, which is used to treat malaria. Digitalis, a substance made from foxgloves, is used to treat heart disease. Rheumatism may be treated with medicine made from the autumn crocus, and leukemia with medicine made from periwinkle.

Periwinkle

Autumn crocus

Cinchona

Foxglove

DISCOVER IT YOURSELF!

Potatoes are good to eat because they are full of starch, which provides energy.

Pile of earth

1. In the spring, dig a patch of ground and plant a potato tuber that has begun to sprout.

2. When the shoot is about 6 inches (15 cm) tall, pile up some earth around the stem. Continue to do this as the plant grows.

3. Late in the summer, the plant will begin to die and you can dig up the new potatoes. Use a fork, but be careful not to spike any potatoes.

Potato tuber

Trees

Forests are very important because trees absorb carbon dioxide and produce oxygen. Unfortunately, many forests have been felled for their wood and many types of trees are in danger of dying out. Wood is a versatile material that is used for fuel, timber, and furniture. Two of the most prized woods for furniture making—teak and mahogany—come from rain forests.

Eye Spy

Many household items are made of wood. How many examples can you find? Look at the color and the grain of the wood. Can you guess what type of tree it came from?

Oldest Trees

Some of the oldest trees in the world are the ancient bristlecone pines, which are found in the United States. They may be as much as 5,000 years old.

What Type of Tree?

Conifers produce cones and have needle-like leaves that stay on the tree all year round. Deciduous trees usually have broad leaves and drop them in the fall.

Deciduous

Conifer

You can learn a lot about a tree by taking a few measurements.

1. Wrap a tape measure around the trunk of a tree about 3 feet (1 m) above the ground.

2. Make a note of the measurement in inches or centimeters. This is the circumference. Divide the circumference by 2.5. This gives you the age of the tree in years.

Bud scale scar

Amount of growth in one year

3. Look for bud scale scars on a twig of the tree. The distance between two bud scale scars is the amount of growth produced by the tree in any one year.

Annual Rings

When you look at a tree stump, you can see growth rings. There is one for each year of the tree's life. By counting the rings, you can determine the age of the tree. In a good year, a tree will lay down a wider ring than in a poor year. By studying the rings, biologists can figure out what the weather was like in the past.

Plants in the Desert

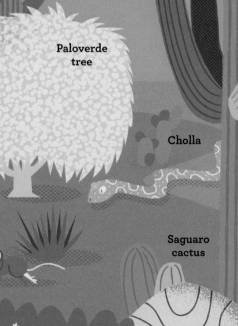

After rain, seeds in the desert soil germinate and a carpet of flowers appears. The flowers quickly produce seeds.

Deserts are dry places that receive very little rain. Daytime temperatures can soar to 86°F (30°C), but at night the lack of clouds means that the temperature may fall to 32°F (0°C). Few plants can survive such harsh conditions, and those that do are specially adapted. Cacti have thick, waxy stems to retain water and spines to deter predators. Other plants appear if there is rain and live for just a few weeks.

Paloverde tree

Cholla

Saguaro cactus

Creosote bush

DISCOVER IT YOURSELF!

!

Cacti are easy to grow, and you can keep several types in a small bowl.

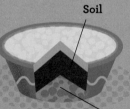

Soil

Pebbles

1. Put a layer of pebbles or gravel at the bottom of a bowl, then fill it with sandy potting soil.

2. Plant your cacti and finish off with a layer of gravel. Give your cacti a little water and place the bowl near a sunny window.

Flowers

Flowers contain a plant's reproductive organs. Most plants have both male and female organs in the same flower, but a few have separate male and female flowers. Male organs, or stamens, make a powdery yellow dust called pollen. Female organs include the stigma and ovary. To make a seed, pollen has to travel to the stigma in another flower. This process is called pollination.

Where Do Our Garden Flowers Come From?

Many garden flowers have been bred from wild flowers. The wild pansy has a small flower, but the garden pansy produces large, brightly colored flowers.

Wild pansy

Garden pansy

Clover

Buttercup

Daisy

Knapweed

Petal Stigma Stamen

Poppy

Corn
marigold

Vetch

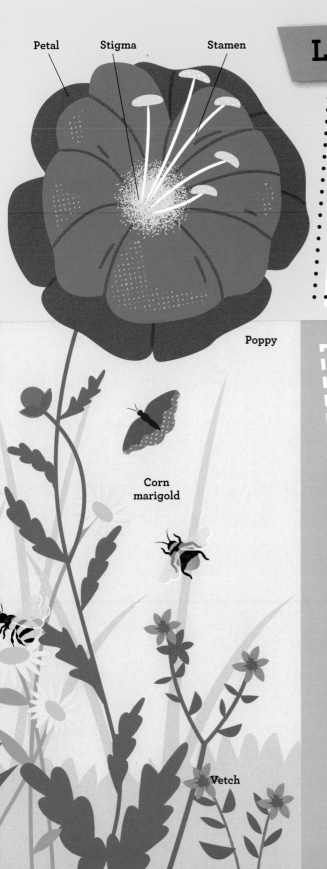

Largest Flower

The rafflesia plant has the largest and smelliest flower of all! For pollination, it attracts flies by creating the smell of rotting flesh.

DISCOVER IT YOURSELF!
Pressed flowers are great for greeting cards.

1. Lay a sheet of watercolor paper on a piece of wood or thick cardboard. Position the flowers on the paper so that they do not touch. Put a second piece of watercolor paper on top, and then another piece of wood and some heavy books.

2. Leave the flowers for several weeks until they are completely dry. Carefully lift the flowers from the watercolor paper.

Wood

Watercolor paper

Wood

23

Look-alikes

The flower of a bee orchid looks just like a bee. This disguise is so lifelike that real bees are encouraged to visit the flower and, in doing so, pick up the pollen.

Plants need help in transporting pollen from the male stamens to the female stigma. Bright colors help this process by telling birds and insects that there is sugary nectar inside the flower. As they collect the nectar, they brush against the stamens and become covered in pollen. When they visit another flower, the pollen is rubbed off onto its stigma, completing pollination. Once the pollen is on the stigma, it grows a tube down the ovary, fertilizing the plant.

Hummingbirds visit flowers to feed on nectar. While they are doing this, their long beaks become covered in pollen, which they then carry to other flowers.

DISCOVER IT YOURSELF!

Find out which colors insects prefer.

1. You will need four pieces of paper, each a different color. On the center of each piece, place an upturned lid.

2. Pour some sugar solution (sugar dissolved in a little water) into the lids. The insects will soon come.

3. Stay close by and tally how many flies land on each color. This will let you know which color flowers insects prefer.

Paper

Upturned lid

Sugar solution

Wind-Blown Pollen

Some flowers rely on the wind to carry pollen. These catkins are groups of male flowers. Each catkin releases up to five million pollen grains to make sure that some of the pollen is carried by the wind to the female flowers.

Eye Spy

How many different types of flowers can you find? Count the petals.

Honeysuckle

Campion

Lupine

Wild rose

Dandelion

See if the petals are joined together to form a tube, like the lupine, or arranged in a circle, like the campion.

Fruits and Seeds

Once a flower has been pollinated, it can make seeds. First the petals and stamens wither and drop off. Then the ovary swells in size and starts to change into a fruit. The seeds develop inside the fruit. A seed has a hard outer covering called the testa. Inside there is a food supply and an embryo that will grow into a new plant.

Cones

Conifers produce cones instead of flowers. The cones contain seeds. As the cone dries out, the scales open and the seeds are blown away.

Eye Spy

A fruit contains seeds, while a vegetable comes from the leaves, roots, or stem. How many different fruits and vegetables can you think of?

In the fall, some plants produce colorful berries that are eaten by birds. Others produce light fruit with fluffy hairs that can float away on the wind.

Clematis

Rose hip

Hawthorn

DISCOVER IT YOURSELF!

Cones make wonderful Christmas decorations.

1. Collect some cones from a local park. Make sure they are dry.

2. Dab a little glue on each cone. Sprinkle it with silver or gold glitter, or spray it with silver or gold paint.

3. Tie some string around the cone and hang it from a Christmas tree. To make a larger decoration, hang three or four cones together.

4. You can also make table decorations using cones, holly, and red ribbon.

Blackberry

Rowan

Elderberry

The Biggest Seed

The fruit of the coco-de-mer weighs up to 40 pounds (18 kg) and contains one seed. The seed can take up to 10 years to develop.

Plants have many clever ways of making sure that their seeds spread far and wide. Some plants produce fruit seeds with hairy parachutes, which carry the seeds on the wind. Others have pods that act like slings, catapulting seeds far away from the parent plant. Spiky fruits get tangled in animal fur. Brightly colored fruits are very tasty, so they are eaten by mammals and birds.

Broom and vetch pods dry and split open, popping out the seeds. The burdock relies on animals to pick up its prickly burs. The seeds of the dandelion, clematis, and sycamore maple are blown by the wind.

Coconut trees are a common sight on tropical beaches. Their fruits drop into the water and are carried by ocean currents to other shores. There they germinate and grow into trees.

Edible Fruits

Brightly colored fruits are sweet-tasting so that they will be eaten by animals. The seeds are passed out in the animal's droppings and dispersed over a large area.

Broom

Burdock

Dandelion

Eye Spy

How many different ways of dispersing can you find among the flowers growing in your yard or local park?

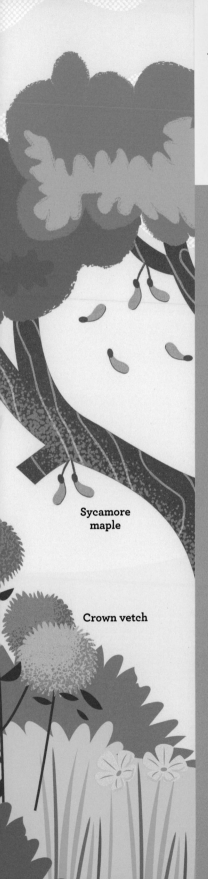

Sycamore maple

Crown vetch

DISCOVER IT YOURSELF!

Pumpkins are very large fruits that you can grow yourself. At Halloween it is fun to hollow one out and put a candle inside.

!

1. Choose a sunny patch in your garden. Mix plenty of compost into the soil to provide nutrients for the plant. Sow the seeds in late spring. As the plant grows, make sure it has plenty of water.

2. The plant will produce separate male and female flowers.

3. To get fruits, you may have to pollinate the female flower, which is the one with swellings behind the petals. Use a small paint brush to pick up pollen from the stamens of the male flower and rub it onto the stigma in the middle of the female flower. Leave only one fruit on the plant so that you get a big pumpkin.

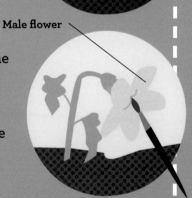

Seed

Male flower

The largest pumpkin ever weighed 883.8 pounds (400.9 kg)!

Starting a New Life

A plant begins its life when the seed germinates. First the seed absorbs water and swells, causing the seed coat to split open. Inside, the embryo has begun to grow. The root is the first to appear, quickly followed by the shoot. Seeds need the right conditions to germinate. Some tree seeds germinate only after many weeks of cold weather. Some seeds survive for many years in the ground, waiting for the right temperature or rain.

A seed swells in size and splits the seed coat. Then the first root appears and anchors the seed in the soil. The shoot arches upward, pulling the seed leaves with it. Above the soil, the shoot straightens and the leaves open. Now the seedlings can photosynthesize.

Eye Spy

Find a tree standing on its own in a park and look around the base for seedlings. Are there more on one side than the other?

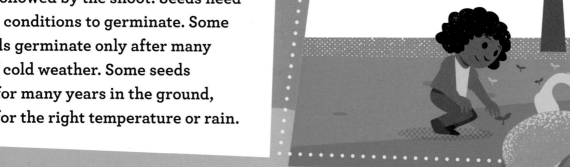

1. Make a few drainage holes in two plastic tubs. Put a paper towel in the bottom and soak it with water. Sprinkle in some garden cress seeds.

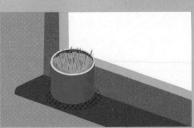

2. Put one tub in the refrigerator and the other on a sunny window ledge.

3. Leave them for a few days, but make sure that they do not dry out. Add more water if necessary.

? How It Works

You should find that the seeds on the window ledge germinate but those in the refrigerator do not. This is because cress seeds need warm conditions to germinate.

After the Fire

The seeds of the banksia plant from Australia only germinate after they have experienced high temperatures and smoke from a fire. After a fire there are nutrients in the ground from the ash and no other plants to compete with.

Index